# FLOWER WREATH HILL: LATER POEMS

# BOOKS BY KENNETH REXROTH

POEMS
    The Collected Shorter Poems
    The Collected Longer Poems
    Sky Sea Birds Trees Earth House Beasts Flowers
    Flower Wreath Hill: Later Poems
    Selected Poems

PLAYS
    Beyond the Mountains

CRITICISM & ESSAYS
    Classics Revisited
    More Classics Revisited
    World Outside the Window: Selected Essays

TRANSLATIONS
    100 Poems from the Chinese
    100 More Poems from the Chinese
    14 Poems of O. V. Lubicz-Milosz
    Seasons of Sacred Lust: The Selected Poems of Kazuko Shiraishi
        *(with Ikuko Atsumi, John Solt, Carol Tinker, and Yasuyo Morita)*
    Women Poets of Japan *(with Ikuko Atsumi)*
    Women Poets of China *(with Ling Chung)*
    Poems from the Greek Anthology
    100 Poems from the Japanese
    100 More Poems from the Japanese
    Selected Poems of Pierre Reverdy
    Li Ch'ing-chao: Complete Poems *(with Ling Chung)*


AUTOBIOGRAPHY
    An Autobiographical Novel

KENNETH REXROTH

# FLOWER
# WREATH
# HILL

LATER POEMS

A NEW DIRECTIONS BOOK

Grateful acknowledgment is made to the various presses that first printed separate sections of this collection: *Sky, Sea, Birds, Trees, Earth, House, Beasts, Flowers* was originally published in a limited edition in 1971 by Unicorn Press; *The Silver Swan* was first published by Copper Canyon Press, Port Townsend, Washington; *On Flower Wreath Hill* by Blackfish Press, Burnaby, British Columbia; and *The Love Poems of Marichiko* by Christopher's Books, Santa Barbara, California.

Acknowledgment is also due to the following publications in which some of the poems in this volume were originally included: *American Poetry Review, Invisible City, Kyoto Review, Poetry Now, Zero* and *New Directions in Prose and Poetry* 26 and 29.

Manufactured in the United States of America
New Directions books are printed on acid-free paper.
First published in the United States as New Directions Paperbook 724 in 1991
Published simultaneously in Canada by Penguin Books Canada Limited

Publisher's note: *Flower Wreath Hill: Later Poems* combines two earlier New Directions editions, *New Poems* (1974) and *The Morning Star* (1979).

Library of Congress Cataloging-in-Publication Data

Rexroth, Kenneth, 1905-1982
    [New poems.   1991]
    Flower Wreath Hill : later poems / Kenneth Rexroth.
       p.   cm.
    Combines two volumes, New poems, and The morning star.
    Includes indexes.
    ISBN 0-8112-1178-9 (pbk. : alk. paper)
    I. Rexroth, Kenneth, 1905-1982   Morning star.  1991.  II. Title.
PS3535.E923A6   1991
811'.52—dc20                    91-18661
                                     CIP

New Directions Books are published for James Laughlin
by New Directions Publishing Corporation,
80 Eighth Avenue, New York 10011

# CONTENTS

# NEW POEMS

For Carol

# LOVE IS AN ART OF TIME

## NOW THE STARLIT MOONLESS SPRING

Now the starlit moonless Spring
Night stands over the Fontaine
De Medicis, and the gold
Fish swim in the cold, starlit
Water. Yesterday, in the
New sunshine, lovers sat by
The water, and talked, and fed
The goldfish, and kissed each other.
I am in California
And evening is coming on.
Now it is morning in Paris
By the Fontaine de Medicis.
And the lovers will come today,
And talk and kiss, and feed the fish,
After they have had their coffee.

# THE FAMILY

Late night
Coming back to Melbourne
From a party on the Kangaroo Plains,
We stop the car by a black pool.
The air is immobile, crystalline.
I get out, light a match,
And study my star map.
I blow out the match,
And overhead and before and below me,
Doubled in the unmoving water,
The million stars come on
That I have never seen before
And will never see again.
And there are the two
Daughter universes of my universe,
The Magellanic Clouds—
Two phosphorescent amoebas overhead,
And two in the bottomless water.

# NO WORD

The trees hang silent
In the heat . . . . .

        Undo your heart
        Tell me your thoughts
        What you were
        And what you are . . . . .

                Like bells no one
                Has ever rung.

# SCHATTEN KUESSE,
# SCHATTEN LIEBE

*after Heine*

Shadow kisses, shadow love,
There is nothing else left now—
Faint electric traces
In the nerve cells of two brains.

The rain falls in the deep night—
Black streets, a distant city—
Far away, too far away—
Yes? Too far away from where?

Too far from time which passes?
Too far from flesh breaking change?
Too far from happiness
Which would not wait an instant?

Two heads alone in dark rooms,
Far apart in rainy night,
Shelter sparks of memory,
Lamps once blazing with kisses.

# HAPAX

*The Same Poem Over and Over*


Holy Week. Once more the full moon
Blooms in deep heaven
Like a crystal flower of ice.
The wide winter constellations
Set in fog brimming over
The seaward hills. Out beyond them,
In the endless dark, uncounted
Minute clots of light go by,
Billions of light years away,
Billions of universes,
Full of stars and their planets
With creatures on them swarming
Like all the living cells on the earth.
They have a number, and I hold
Their being and their number
In one suety speck of jelly
Inside my skull. I have seen them
Swimming in the midst of rushing
Infinite space, through a lens of glass
Through a lens of flesh, on a cup of nerves.
The question is not
Does being have meaning,
But does meaning have being.
What is happening?
All day I walk over ridges
And beside cascades and pools
Deep into the Spring hills.
Mushrooms come up in the same spot
In the abandoned clearing.
Trillium and adder's tongue
Are in place by the waterfall.

A heron lifts from a pool
As I come near, as it has done
For forty years, and flies off
Through the same gap in the trees.
The same rush and lift of flapping wings,
The same cry, how many
Generations of herons?
The same red tailed hawks court each other
High on the same rising air
Above a grassy steep. Squirrels leap
In the same oaks. Back at my cabin
In the twilight an owl on the same
Limb moans in his ancient language.
Billions and billions of worlds
Full of beings larger than dinosaurs
And smaller than viruses, each
In its place, the ecology
Of infinity.
I look at the rising Easter moon.
The flowering madrone gleams in the moonlight.
The bees in the cabin wall
Are awake. The night is full
Of flowers and perfume and honey.
I can see the bees in the moonlight
Flying to the hole under the window,
Glowing faintly like the flying universes.
What does it mean. This is not a question, but
    an exclamation.

# CONFUSION OF THE SENSES

Moonlight fills the laurels
Like music. The moonlit
Air does not move. Your white
Face moves towards my face.
Voluptuous sorrow
Holds us like a cobweb
Like a song, a perfume, the moonlight.
Your hair falls and holds our faces.
Your lips curl into mine.
Your tongue enters my mouth.
A bat flies through the moonlight.
The moonlight fills your eyes
They have neither iris nor pupil
They are only globes of cold fire
Like the deers' eyes that go by us
Through the empty forest.
Your slender body quivers
And smells of seaweed.
We lie together listening
To each other breathing in the moonlight.
Do you hear? We are breathing. We are alive.

# BLUE SUNDAY

Chestnut flowers are falling
In the empty street that smells
Of hospitals and cooking.
The radio is breaking
Somebody's heart somewhere
In a dirty bedroom. Nobody
Is listening. For ten miles
In either direction
There are no spots on the dice.
The houses are all empty.
Nobody lives in this city.
Outside the city limits
Are green and white cemeteries.
Nobody is in the graves.
At very long intervals
The broken cast iron fountain
In the courtyard sneezes and spurts.
In the dirty bedroom
Three young whores are shooting dice.
At very long intervals
One of them speaks to the dice.
Otherwise they are silent.
After the chestnut blossoms
Have all fallen the yellow
Sun will set and stars shine
Over the empty city
And papers blow down the street.

# I DREAM OF LESLIE

You entered my sleep,
Come with your immense,
Luminous eyes,
And light brown hair,
Across fifty years,
To sing for me again that song
Of Campion's we loved so once.
I kissed your quivering throat.
There was no hint in the dream
That you were long, long since
A new arrivéd guest,
With blithe Helen, white Iope and the rest—
Only the peace
Of late afternoon
In a compassionate autumn
In youth.
And I forgot
That I was old and you a shade.

# EDUCATION

Now to the dry hillside,
Terraced with crumbling limestone,
Where there were vineyards long ago,
Evening comes cool and violet
Under the olive trees, and only
The almond blossoms and the first stars
Are alight. Your fine lean hand
Like a spindle of light
Moves as you talk, as if
You were conducting a slow music.
What are you talking about?
You are explaining everything to me—
The abandoned olive grove,
The walls older than the Romans,
The flowering almond tree,
And the twilight darkening
Around the stars and around
You speaking lips and moving hand.

# PRIVACY

Dense fog shuts down
Between the hills.
I step out of my cabin.
You'd never know
It was in the midst of a forest.
Fog curls in the lighted doorway like smoke.
I hear the raccoon rustling
In the invisible thicket.
The cool dampness creeps under my clothes.
I thought I heard a car
Come up the road below me.
I walk cautiously through the fog
To the edge of the cutting.
I can see nothing.
Suddenly I hear
Beneath my feet
A man and a woman cry out with love.

# PARITY

My uncle believed he had
A double in another
Universe right here at hand
Whose life was the opposite
Of his in all things—the man
On the other side of zero.
Sometimes they would change places.
Not in dreams, but for a moment
In waking, when my uncle
Would smile a certain sly smile
And pause or stagger slightly
And go about his business.

# IT IS A GERMAN HONEYMOON

They are stalking humming birds
The jewels of the new world
The rufous hummingbird dives
Along his parabola
Of pure ether. We forgot—
An imponderable and
Invisible elastic
Crystal is the womb of space.
They wait with poised cameras
Focused telescopic lens
Beyond the crimson trumpet vine.
He returns squealing against
The sky deeper than six billion
Light years, and plunges through sun
Blaze to the blood red flower womb.
A whirling note in the lens of space.
"Birds are devas," says Morris
Graves, "They live in a world
Without Karma." No grasping,
No consequence, only the
Grace of the vectors that form
The lattices of the unending
Imponderable crystal.
The blond and handsome young man
And woman are happy, they
Love each other, when they have
Gone around the world they will
Sit in the Grunewald and
Look at a picture of a
California hummingbird.
Nobody can swim across
The Great River. Turn your back
And study the spotted wall.
Turn around on the farther shore.
Nine dice roll out, one by one.

The mouse eats them. They never were.
The hundred flowers put their
Heads together, yellow stamens and
Swelling pistils. Between them
In midspace they generate
A single seed. You cannot
Find it in a telescope.
Found, you could not see it in
An electron microscope.

# BEI WANNSEE

Evening twirling
In a thousand thanks
The spindle glows
Pale water
Copper flows
Swans
Sails cluster and part again
Ripples
Mouths kiss and suck and part
The sun breaks in bands of haze
A silent exclamation
A white bird
A naked joy
A thousand thanks
The water becomes imaginary
The swans go
The lights come
Paler than water
The perfume of the bed of stock
Billows down the lawn and out
Over the water
Past the motionless scarves of weeping willow
And up from the glittering boat
A flute spirals and says quietly
Like a waving light

A blonde

Come

A thousand thanks
A waving light.

# RED MAPLE LEAVES

The maple leaves are brilliant
Over the tree lined streets.
The deep shade is filled
With soft ruddy light.
Soon the leaves will all have fallen.
The pale winter sunlight
Will gleam on snow covered lawns.
Here we were young together
And loved each other
Wise beyond our years.
Two lifetimes have gone by.
Only us two are left from those days.
All the others have gone with the years.
We have never seen each other since.
This is the first time I have ever come back.
I drive slowly past your home,
Around the block again and once again.
Beyond the deep pillared porch
Someone is sitting at the window.
I drive down by the river
And watch a boy fishing from the bridge
In the clear water amongst
Falling and floating leaves.
And then I drive West into the smoky sunset.

# IT TURNS OVER

The lightning does not go out
But stays on in the sky all night
A waterfall of solid white fire
Red hands speak
In deaf and dumb language
Their green shadows
Projected on the orange sky
All the worms come out
All the eggs hatch
All the clouds boil away
Only Orion all alone in the zenith
Of midsummer midnight.

# STAR AND CRESCENT

The air has the late summer
Evening smell of ripe foliage
And dew cooled dust. The last long
Rays of sunset have gone from
The sky. In the greying light
The last birds twitter in the leaves.
Far away through the trees, someone
Is pounding something. The new
Moon is pale and thin as a
Flake of ice. Venus glows warm
Beside it. In the abode
Of peace, a bell calls for
Evening meditation.
As the twilight deepens
A voice speaks in the silence.

## LA VIE EN ROSE

Fog fills the little square
Between Avenue du Maine
And the Gaité Montparnasse.
I walk around and around,
Waiting for my girl.
My footsteps echo
From the walls
Of the second storeys.
Deep in the future
My ghost follows me,
Around and around.

# VOID ONLY

Time like glass
Space like glass
I sit quiet
Anywhere Anything
Happens
Quiet loud still turbulent
The serpent coils
On itself
All things are translucent
Then transparent
Then gone
Only emptiness
No limits
Only the infinitely faint
Song
Of the coiling mind
Only.

# SUCHNESS

In the theosophy of light,
The logical universal
Ceases to be anything more
Than the dead body of an angel.
What is substance? Our substance
Is whatever we feed our angel.
The perfect incense for worship
Is camphor, whose flames leave no ashes.

# LATE HALF MOON

Late half moon
High over head.
Shaka merges with Tara.
The dark bride possesses her lover.
Two moaning owls fly from the
Pine to the cypress.
The largest telescope
Reveals more nebulae
Outside our galaxy
Than stars within it—
There are more cells
In a single brain.
The sands of all the seas
Have a number.
The red shift—
The mortal soul
In its immortal body.
Light tires and wears out,
Travelling through space.
The owls mate
In the moonfilled dawn.

# YOUR BIRTHDAY IN THE CALIFORNIA MOUNTAINS

A broken moon on the cold water,
And wild geese crying high overhead,
The smoke of the campfire rises
Toward the geometry of heaven—
Points of light in the infinite blackness.
I watch across the narrow inlet
Your dark figure comes and goes before the fire.
A loon cries out on the night bound lake.
Then all the world is silent with the
Silence of autumn waiting for
The coming of winter. I enter
The ring of firelight, bringing to you
A string of trout for our dinner.
As we eat by the whispering lake,
I say, "Many years from now we will
Remember this night and talk of it."
Many years have gone by since then, and
Many years again. I remember
That night as though it was last night,
But you have been dead for thirty years.

## THE FLOWER SUTRA

Deep drowsy shade under the broad leaves,
The dusty plain far below dim with haze,
Picking flowers—bush clover, gold banded lily,
Bell flower, wild pink, while a mountain cuckoo
Flutters about, watching me and crying,
"Kegonkyo."

## EARTH SKY SEA
## TREES BIRDS
## HOUSE
## BEASTS FLOWERS

*Cold before dawn*

Cold before dawn,
Off in the misty night,
Under the gibbous moon,
The peacocks cry to each other,
As if in pain.

*A cottage in the midst*

A cottage in the midst
Of a miniature forest.
The only events are the distant
Cries of peacocks, the barking
Of more distant dogs
And high over head
The flight of cawing crows.

*Past and future fall away*

Past and future fall away.
There is only the rose and blue
Shimmer of the illimitable
Sea surface.
No place.
No time.

*Slowly the moon rises*

Slowly the moon rises
Over the quiet sea.
Slowly the face of my beloved
Forms in my mind.

*Moonless night*

Moonless night.
In the black heavens
The eye goes ten million miles.
Melancholy fills the heart.

## Spring puddles give way

Spring puddles give way
To young grass.
In the garden, willow catkins
Change to singing birds.


## A dawn in a tree of birds

A dawn in a tree of birds.
Another.
And then another.


## Past midnight

Past midnight,
In the dark,
Under the winter stars,
Tendrils of ice
Creep through the duckweed.

## As *the years pass*

As the years pass,
The generations of birds pass too.
But you must watch carefully.
The same towhees and jays
Seem to have been in the same places
To thousands of generations of men.

## *In the dark forest the whisper*

In the dark forest the whisper
Of a million leaves.
On the deep sea the sigh
Of a million waves.

## A *long lifetime*

A long lifetime
Peoples and places
And the crisis of mankind—
What survives is the crystal—
Infinitely small—
Infinitely large—

# THE CITY OF THE MOON

for *Kimiko Nakazawa*

### I

The sun sets as the moon
Rises. The red maple leaves
Fade to the color
Of an aging heart.

### II

In the fine warm rain
Falling over the late turning
Maple leaves, an uguisu
Sings as if in Spring.

### III

The East Wind brings clouds
And rain. In the ruffled pond
Happy goldfish play.
But it is the end
Of the eleventh month, warm,
Unseasonably.

### IV

Although I am far from home
The red maple leaves
Over the old pond
Of the temple garden
Are falling with the
Plum leaves by my own window.

## V

No, I did not say a word.
It is useless to
Pretend that the sound of rain
Is a human voice.

I shall have the banana
Trees by my window destroyed.
The pattering of
The rain sounds like the weeping
Of all the spirits
Of the air, and the
Wind tearing the leaves sounds like
The sound of ripped silk.

## VI

In a waking dream,
A princess of the old time
Comes to me over
The twisting foot bridge,
Through the midst of the marsh
Of yellow iris
And lightly touches my lips.
The delicate sensation
Of utter intimacy
Lingers as the light goes out,
And the leaves of the iris
Murmur and rustle
In the twilight wind.

## VII

Although the great plane
Flies away toward the sun,
The morning raven
Will still perch on the balcony
Of the Ueno Park of the heart.


## VIII

### THE NEW YEAR

Midnight passes—
A new year—Orion strides
Into the warm waves
Westward to Yamashina
Where the red and gold
Of a glorious autumn
Lie under the snow.


## IX

### ICHŌ

The plane rises through
Snowing clouds. Far beneath two
Autumn ginkos blaze,
Burning gold in the harsh
Night lights of Tokyo.

## X

Buddha took some Autumn leaves
In his hand and asked
Ananda if these were all
The red leaves there were.
Ananda answered that it
Was Autumn and leaves
Were falling all about them,
More than could ever
Be numbered. So Buddha said,
"I have given you
A handful of truths. Besides
These there are many
Thousands of other truths, more
Than can ever be numbered."


## XI

Clouds are the thoughts of
Heaven. It is difficult
To read the thoughts of
Other people, but you can
Always read those of heaven.

*Kyoto*
*November 1972*

# IMITATIONS OF THE CHINESE

for Ling

# THE FALL OF CH'OU

Jade pendants chime before the dawn audience.
Peach blossoms drown in the swollen stream.
Barbarian fires overwhelm the guards.
Together two skylarks rise towards heaven.
Two hearts singing like chiming jade.


# ERINNERUNG

At the door of my thatched hut,
Buried deep in the forested mountains,
The wind in the ancient ginko tree
Sounds like the rustle of brocaded silk.

## LOST LOVE

Geese fly from North to South
You are far away in
The East. The West wind will carry
A message to the East, but
Here in the Far West, the East
Wind never blows.

# MORE TRANSLATIONS

## FROM THE CHINESE

# THE CHERRY TREE

The cherry as spring comes on
Will bloom again by the same pool.
Man keeps the love of the years that are gone
The flowers return to the same branches.

*Anonymous*

# A RINGING BELL

I lie in my bed,
Listening to the monastery bell.
In the still night
The sound re-echoes amongst the hills.
Frost gathers under the cold moon.
Under the overcast sky,
In the depths of the night,
The first tones are still reverberating
While the last tones are ringing clear and sharp.
I listen and I can still hear them both,
But I cannot tell when they fade away.
I know the bondage and vanity of the world.
But who can tell when we escape
From life and death?

*Ch'ang Yu*

# THANK YOU FOR
# YOUR LETTER

The letter you sent me touched my heart.
The paper was decorated with a pair of magpies.
Now I think always of the magpies who fly with joined wings.
I do not mind that your letter was so short.

*The Poetess Ch'ao Li-houa*


# THE FIREFLIES DANCE
# IN THE DARK

The fireflies dance in the dark
Like sparkling atoms.
The last song of the crickets
In the evening
Awakes all the old memories.
Suddenly the moon vanishes
Behind the roof top.
The wind growls in the stove.
Threads of frost crystals
Appear on the cold bamboo leaves.

*Emperor Ch'ien-wen of Liang*

# GETTING UP IN WINTER

Winter morning.
Pale sunlight strikes the ceiling.
She gets out of bed reluctantly.
Her nightgown has a bamboo sash.
She wipes the dew off her mirror.
At this hour there is no one to see her.
Why is she making up so early?

*Emperor Ch'ien-wen of Liang*


# AUTUMN

A cup of clear wine
Sweet as honey.
A girl with braids
Black as a crow,
Why ask if Spring
Is lovelier than Autumn?
I have never been able
To decide if peach blossoms
Were prettier than chrysanthemums.

*Ch'in Kuan*

# SPRING

Light clouds, high noon,
Beautiful weather.
There is no wind
In the old willow tree.
The blue green jade leaves
Are perfectly still.
I read lazily,
Scratching my head.
Beyond the wall
I can hear
Now and then
The flute of a cakeseller.

*Ch'in Kuan*


# ALONG THE GRAND CANAL

Hoar frost has congealed
On the deck
Of my little boat.
The water
Is clear and still.
Cold stars beyond counting
Swim alongside.
Thick reeds hide the shore.
You'd think you'd left the earth.
Suddenly there breaks in
Laughter and song.

*Ch'in Kuan*

# SPRING BEGINS

Golden murmur of new poplar leaves
On the swaying branches.
The Spring breeze blows through the painted hall.
My head clears from wine.
I lay aside my fan
And sing softly to myself.
New snow blows through the bamboo blinds—
But it smells to me like peach blossoms.

*Ch'in Kuan*


# STROLLING IN THE MOONLIGHT

Me and my cane, that's two of us.
We walk in the moonlight.
Our shadow makes three.
I don't know where my family
Have all gone to.
Now that I am old
I'll have to take care of myself.

*Ch'in Kuan*

# SORROW

I grew up without the care of parents.
My heart is shut away in its sorrow.
Already my hair is turning grey
And I wander all alone in an empty house.
My life has been so hard and troubled
It is difficult for me to tell it over.
When I was seventeen I lost my husband
At eighteen my only son died.
Now they sleep forever in the cemetery
Under the weeping willows
Under summer dew and winter snow.
Under roofs of grass and weeds.
Why are our lives so unequal?
Why is the will of heaven so capricious?
There is no one but myself to comfort me.
People avoid me because of my sadness.
I watch the birds roosting together on the same branch
And I can never put my empty nest out of my mind.

*The Poetess Fang Wei-yi*

# OVER

In the old days,
You and me,
We were close as a man and his shadow.
Now when you are with me,
You are vague as a cloud.

In the old days,
You and me
We were like a song and its echo, one to the other.
Now when you are with me
We are like dead leaves falling from the branch.

In the old days,
You and me,
We were like gold in quartz, without spot or blemish.
Now when you are with me
We are like dead stars whose splendor is long gone.

*Fou Hinan*

# HOPELESSNESS

When I look in the mirror
My face frightens me.
How horrible I have become!
When Spring comes back
Weakness overcomes me
Like a fatal sickness.
I am too slothful
To smell the new flowers
Or to powder my own face.
Everything exasperates me.
The sadness which tries me today
Adds itself to the accumulated
Sorrows of the days that are gone.
I am frightened by the weird cries
Of the nightjars that I cannot
Shut out from my ears.
I am filled with bitter embarrassment
When I see on the curtains
The shadows of two swallows making love.

*Li Ch'ing-chao*

# DEEP NIGHT

Deep night. I sing, alone in the dark.
The music of the strings reveals my heart.
Frost creeps through the curtains of the bed.
The wind rustles in the trees.
The bright lamp has gone out.
The bright face is gone forever.
I sing your poems
To the tunes you used to sing.
Now the music brings only the deepest sorrow.

*Pao Ch'ao*


# SINCE YOU WENT AWAY

After you were gone
The moon came and shone
In the vacant window.
I thought of you as a flower
Carried off by the wind,
That went its way,
And can never turn back.

*The Poetess Shu Ch'i-siang*

## DRINKING ON THE LAKE,
## FAIR WEATHER, THEN RAIN

Light floods the waves
It is a beautiful day.
Suddenly dark clouds
Hide the mountains.
The rain is refreshing, too.
Lake of the West, Lady of the West—
They are incomparable.
Lightly painted, heavily made up
I find most girls equally attractive.

*Su Tung P'o*

## ON A PAINTING BY WANG,
## THE CLERK OF YEN LING

The slender bamboo is like a hermit.
The simple flower is like a maiden.
The sparrow tilts on the branch.
A gust of rain sprinkles the flowers.
He spreads his wings to fly
And shakes all the leaves.
The bees gathering honey
Are trapped in the nectar.
What a wonderful talent
That can create an entire Spring
With a brush and a sheet of paper.
If he would try poetry
I know he would be a master of words.

*Su Tung P'o*


## FLOWER PETALS DRIFT
## OVER THE COURTYARD

Flower petals drift over the courtyard
Moss creeps into the rooms
Everything was said on both sides
Now there is only a musty smell in the air.

*Wang Ch'ang-ling*

# COMPLAINT OF A YOUNG GIRL

Nobody but me can know the sorrow that wrings me.
Weeping I return to my obscurity
I keep from the past only bitterness
In the present there is only black emptiness.

I send you back your gifts, jewels, earrings,
The fur jacket I wore in the old days,
You can tie up a broken string
But never put back together a broken heart.

*Wang Chung-ju*

# THINKING OF HIS DEAD WIFE

The autumn winds begin.
White clouds drift across the sky.
The leaves turn yellow and fall.
Wild geese pass over head towards the South.
Autumn iris are in bud.
Chrysanthemums start to bloom.
I think of the girl I love
Who I can never forget.
I take the ferry boat
Across the turbulent river.
The prow plunges in the current,
Through the foaming waves.
I listen to the flutes and drums.
I listen to the songs of the rowers.
Everybody is so happy.
Only my heart is full of sorrow.
If I cannot bear this when I am strong and young,
What will happen when I grow old?

*Emperor Wu of Han*

# FOR HIS JOYFUL
## HOMECOMING

For his joyful homecoming
I put on my embroidered girdle
Over my brocade dress
Decorated with symbols of faithful love.
Full of passion he came
On the night of the full moon.
Laughing, we played at clouds and rain
Until the sun came up.

*Emperor Wu of Liang*


# LAST AUTUMN ENDED

Last autumn ended
Just a little while ago.
Now it is the beginning
Of the autumn of another year.
Heavy dewfall,
Cold air drains down the mountain.
Gusts of wind
The nostalgia of the crickets' last song.
Flocks of chattering birds
Prepare to leave our forest.
Soon the fishes will hide
Deep under the waterweeds.
Sometimes the sun breaks through the fog.
Other times the low clouds
Growl with thunder.

*Emperor Yang of Sui*

# CHINESE POEMS

*Translated by Kenneth Rexroth and Ling Chung*

# TRAVELLING IN HSIANG COUNTY

Flying flowers from both shores
Glow red on our boat.
In half a day we speed
100 li between elm lined banks.
I lie and watch the sky
Full of unmoving clouds
And do not realize
Both I and the clouds
Are borne together on the East Wind.

*Ch'en Yu I*

# COMPOSED IN A DREAM

On the road of Spring, rain multiplies the flowers,
And the flowers kindle the mountain into Spring.
I follow the brook to its hidden source
Among a thousand golden orioles.

Before my eyes the flying clouds
Change into dragons dancing in the blue sky.
Drunk, lying in the shade
Of the old rattan blinds,
I can't tell North from South.

*Ch'in Kuan*
*[1048–1100]*

# WRITTEN FOR KO YAH CH'ING

My lord, you live beside the river
In a painted palace
And I live at the corner of the sea.
My tears fall in the sea
And the tide carries them
Before your tower
Where they stop in the flowing water.

*Han Chu*

# WEST VILLAGE

There are temples everywhere
But in West Village
There are only eight or nine families.
I catch some fish,
But there is no place to sell them.
I buy some wine,
And eat and drink
Amongst the flowering rushes.

*Kuo Hsiang Cheng*


# EVENING VIEW FROM
# WILLOW BRIDGE

I hear a fish jump in the little pool.
I wait for my crane
To return from the thick woods.

The idle clouds
Will not make rain
But fly off to
The blue peaks.

*Lu Yu*

# EXILE IN JAPAN

On the balcony of the tower
I play my flute and watch
The Spring rain.
I wonder
If I ever
Will go home and see
The tide bore
In Chekiang River again.
Straw sandals, an old
Begging bowl, nobody
Knows me. On how many
Bridges have I trampled
The fallen cherry blossoms?

*Su Man Shu*


# ON THE RIVER

The West wind ruffles the water
And scatters the last red flowers over the river.
A horizontal flute blows a friend's farewell,
Eastward across the jumbled hills.

*Wang An Shih*

# BOATING ON WU SUNG RIVER

The setting sun leaks through the sparse,
Slender, flowering rushes.
For half a day I've been alone
Chanting poems
And haven't crossed the river.
Only the egrets have understood me.
Time after time they come
Stand on one leg and look in the boat window.

*Wang Yu Ch'en*

# THE MORNING STAR

# THE SILVER SWAN

*poems and translations*
written in Kyoto 1974–1978

# I

for *Ruth Stephan*

Twilit snow,
The last time I saw it
Was with you.
Now you are dead
By your own hand
After great pain.
Twilit snow.


# I I


As the full moon rises
The swan sings
In sleep
On the lake of the mind.

## I I I

Orange and silver
Twilight over Yoshino.
Then the frosty stars,
Moving like crystals against
The wind from Siberia.

## I V

Under the half moon
The field crickets are silent.
Only the cricket
Of the hearth still sings, louder
Still, behind the gas heater.

## V

Late night, under the
Low, waning eleventh month
Moon, wild frosted kaki
On the bare branches gleam like
Pearls. Tomorrow they
Will be sweet as the
Honey of Summer.

## V I

*Asagumori*

On the forest path
The leaves fall. In the withered
Grass the crickets sing
Their last songs. Through dew and dusk
I walk the paths you once walked,
My sleeves wet with memory.

# VII

## Void Only

I cannot escape from you.
When I think I am alone,
I awake to discover
I am lost in the jungle
Of your love, in its darkness
Jewelled with the eyes of unknown
Beasts. I awake to discover
I am a forest ascetic
In the impenetrable
Void only, the single thought
Of which nothing can be said.

# VIII

## Seven Seven

Can I come to you
When the cowboy comes to the
Weaving girl? No sea is as
Wide as the River of Heaven.

## I X

The new moon has reached
The half. It is utterly
Incredible. One
Month ago we were strangers.

## X

*After Akiko*—"Yoru no cho ni"

for *Yasuyo*

In your frost white kimono
Embroidered with bare branches
I walk you home New Year's Eve.
As we pass a street lamp
A few tiny bright feathers
Float in the air. Stars form on
Your wind blown hair and you cry,
"The first snow!"

## XI

Late Spring.
Before he goes, the uguisu
Says over and over again
The simple lesson no man
Knows, because
No man can ever learn.


## XII

Bride and groom,
The moon shines
Above the typhoon.

# XIII

Only the sea mist,
Void only.
Only the rising
Full moon,
Void only.


# XIV

*Hototogisu—horobirete*

The cuckoo's call, though
Sweet in itself, is hard to
Bear, for it cries,
"Perishing! Perishing!"
Against the Spring.

## XV

*Tsukutsukuboshi*

In the month of great heat
The first bell cricket cries.
"It is time to leave."


## XVI

*New Year*

The full moon shines on
The first plum blossoms and opens
The Year of the Dragon.
May happy Dragons
Attend you with gifts of joy.

# XVII

An hour before sunrise,
The moon low in the East,
Soon it will pass the sun.
The Morning Star hangs like a
Lamp, beside the crescent,
Above the greying horizon.
The air warm, perfumed,
An unseasonably warm,
Rainy Autumn, nevertheless
The leaves turn color, contour
By contour down the mountains.
I watch the wavering,
Coiling of the smoke of a
Stick of temple incense in
The rays of my reading lamp.
Moonlight appears on my wall
As though I raised it by
Incantation. I go out
Into the wooded garden
And walk, nude, except for my
Sandals, through light and dark banded
Like a field of sleeping tigers.
Our racoons watch me from the
Walnut tree, the opossums
Glide out of sight under the
Woodpile. My dog Ch'ing is asleep.
So is the cat. I am alone
In the stillness before the
First birds wake. The night creatures
Have all gone to sleep. Blackness
Looms at the end of the garden,
An impenetrable cube.
A ray of the Morning Star
Pierces a shaft of moon-filled mist.
A naked girl takes form
And comes toward me—translucent,
Her body made of infinite

Whirling points of light, each one
A galaxy, like clouds of
Fireflies beyond numbering.
Through them, star and moon
Still glisten faintly. She comes
To me on imperceptibly
Drifting air, and touches me
On the shoulder with a hand
Softer than silk. She says
"Lover, do you know what Heart
You have possessed?"
Before I can answer, her
Body flows into mine, each
Corpuscle of light merges
With a corpuscle of blood or flesh.
As we become one the world
Vanishes. My self vanishes.
I am dispossessed, only
An abyss without limits.
Only dark oblivion
Of sense and mind in an
Illimitable Void.
Infinitely away burns
A minute red point to which
I move or which moves to me.
Time fades away. Motion is
Not motion. Space becomes Void.
A ruby fire fills all being.
It opens, not like a gate,
Like hands in prayer that unclasp
And close around me.
Then nothing. All senses ceased.
No awareness, nothing,
Only another kind of knowing
Of an all encompassing
Love that has consumed all being.
Time has had a stop.
Space is gone.
Grasping and consequence

**Never existed.**
The aeons have fallen away.

Suddenly I am standing
In my garden, nude, bathed in
The hot brilliance of the new
Risen sun—star and crescent gone into light.

## XVIII

Midnight, the waning moon
Of midsummer glows
From the raindrops on
The first flowers of Autumn.

## XIX

The drowned moon plunges
Through a towering surf
Of storm clouds, and momently
The wet leaves glitter.
Moment by moment an owl cries.
Rodents scurry, building
Their winter nests, in the moments of dark.

## XX

Plovers cry in the
Dark over the high moorland,
The overtones of the sea,
Calling deep into the land.

## XXI

Long past midnight, I walk out
In the garden after a
Hot bath, in yukata
And clogs. I feel no cold.
But the leaves have all fallen
From the fruit trees and the
Kaki hang there alone
Filled with frosty moonlight.
Suddenly I am aware
There is no sound
Not of insects nor of frogs nor of birds
Only the slow pulse of
An owl marking time for the silence.

## XXII

Bright in the East
The morrow pure and pale
This hour, this is our last hourglass.
The parting forever of lovers
Is a double suicide
Of the consciousness.
By tens and thousands the stars go out.

# XXIII

*All This to Pass Never to Be Again*

for *Christina, Carol, and Kenneth*

We feed the blue jays
Peanuts from our hands.
As the sun sets, the quarter moon
Shows pale as snow in the orange sky.
While we eat our high cuisine,
The moon, deep in the sky
Moves again in the pool,
And makes it deep as the sky
Where Scorpio moves with it,
Past the South. The crossroads
Of heaven glimmer with billions
Of worlds. The night cools.
We go indoors and talk
Of the wisdom and the
Insoluble problems of India.
Late in the night,
After the moon is down,
Coyotes sing on the hills.
How easy it is to put together
A poem of life lived
Simply and beautifully.
How steadily, as the age grows old,
The opportunity to do so narrows.

## XXIV

Flowers sleep by the window.
The lamp holds fast the light.
Carelessly the window holds back the darkness outside.
The empty picture frames exhibit their contents,
And reflect the motionless flies on the walls.

The flowers hold themselves up against the night.
The lamp spins the night.
The cat in the corner spins the wool of sleep.
On the fire now and then the coffeepot snores with content.
Silent children play with words on the ground.

Set the white table. Wait for someone
Whose footsteps will never come up the stairs.

A train bores through the distant silence,
Never revealing the secret of things.
Destiny counts the clock ticks in decimals.

*Gunnar Ekelof*

## XXV

*October Mirror*

Nerves grind quietly in the twilight
That flows grey and quiet past the window,
When red flowers fade quiet in the twilight
And the lamp sings to itself in the corner.

Silence drinks the quiet Autumn rain
Which no longer means anything to the harvest.
The hands warm their knuckles.
The eyes gaze quiet at the fading embers.

*Gunnar Ekelof*

# XXVI

*Equation*

Only truth can explain your eyes
That sow stars in the vault of heaven,
Where the clouds float through a field of tones

(The flowers which are born out of nothing,
When your eyes make fate so simple,
And the stars fly away from the hive
In the blue-green waiting room of heaven)

And explain your rapport with destiny.

*Gunnar Ekelof*

# XXVII

I look around,
No cherry blossoms,
No maple leaves,
Only a narrow inlet,
A thatched hut,
In the Autumn evening.

*Fujiwara no Teika*

## XXVIII

I wonder if you can know
In the island of
Your heart, deprived of
Food, unable to escape,
How utterly banished I am.

*Yosano Akiko*

# ON FLOWER WREATH HILL

*For Yasuyo Morita*

# I

An aging pilgrim on a
Darkening path walks through the
Fallen and falling leaves, through
A forest grown over the
Hilltop tumulus of a
Long dead princess, as the
Moonlight grows and the daylight
Fades and the Western Hills turn
Dim in the distance and the
Lights come on, pale green
In the streets of the hazy city.

## I I

Who was this princess under
This mound overgrown with trees
Now almost bare of leaves?
Only the pine and cypress
Are still green. Scattered through the
Dusk are orange wild kaki on
Bare branches. Darkness, an owl
Answers the temple bell. The
Sun has passed the crossroads of
Heaven.
     There are more leaves on
The ground than grew on the trees.
I can no longer see the
Path; I find my way without
Stumbling; my heavy heart has
Gone this way before. Until
Life goes out memory will
Not vanish, but grow stronger
Night by night.
          Aching nostalgia—
In the darkness every moment
Grows longer and longer, and
I feel as timeless as the
Two thousand year old cypress.

# III

The full moon rises over
Blue Mount Hiei as the orange
Twilight gives way to dusk.
Kamo River is full with
The first rains of Autumn, the
Water crowded with colored
Leaves, red maple, yellow gingko,
On dark water, like Chinese
Old brocade. The Autumn haze
Deepens until only the
Lights of the city remain.

# I V

No leaf stirs. I am alone
In the midst of a hundred
Empty mountains. Cicadas,
Locusts, katydids, crickets,
Have fallen still, one after
Another. Even the wind
Bells hang motionless. In the
Blue dusk, widely spaced snowflakes
Fall in perfect verticals.
Yet, under my cabin porch,
The thin, clear Autumn water
Rustles softly like fine silk.

# V

This world of ours, before we
Can know its fleeting sorrows,
We enter it through tears.
Do the reverberations
Of the evening bell of
The mountain temple ever
Totally die away?
Memory echoes and reechoes
Always reinforcing itself.
No wave motion ever dies.
The white waves of the wake of
The boat that rows away into
The dawn, spread and lap on the
Sands of the shores of all the world.

## V I

Clustered in the forest around
The royal tumulus are
Tumbled and shattered gravestones
Of people no one left in
The world remembers. For the
New Year the newer ones have all been cleaned
And straightened and each has
Flowers or at least a spray
Of bamboo and pine.
It is a great pleasure to
Walk through fallen leaves, but
Remember, you are alive,
As they were two months ago.

# VII

Night shuts down the misty mountains
With fine rain. The seventh day
Of my seventieth year,
Seven-Seven-Ten, my own
Tanabata, and my own
Great Purification. Who
Crosses in midwinter from
Altair to Vega, from the
Eagle to the Swan, under the earth,
Against the sun? Orion,
My guardian king, stands on
Kegonkyoyama.
So many of these ancient
Tombs are the graves of heroes
Who died young. The combinations
Of the world are unstable
By nature. Take it easy.
Nirvana.
Change rules the world forever.
And man but a little while.

# VIII

Oborozuki,
Drowned Moon,
The half moon is drowned in mist
Its hazy light gleams on leaves
Drenched with warm mist. The world
Is alive tonight. I am
Immersed in living protoplasm,
That stretches away over
Continents and seas. I float
Like a child in the womb. Each
Cell of my body is
Penetrated by a
Strange electric life. I glow
In the dark with the moon drenched
Leaves, myself a globe
Of St. Elmo's fire.

I move silently on the
Wet forest path that circles
The shattered tumulus.
The path is invisible.
I am only a dim glow
Like the tumbled and broken
Gravestones of forgotten men
And women that mark the way.
I sit for a while on one
Tumbled sotoba and listen
To the conversations of
Owls and nightjars and tree frogs.
As my eyes adjust to the
Denser darkness I can see
That my seat is a cube and
All around me are scattered
Earth, water, air, fire, ether.
Of these five elements
The moon, the mist, the world, man
Are only fleeting compounds

Varying in power, and
Power is only insight
Into the void—the single
Thought that illuminates the heart.
The heart's mirror hangs in the void.

Do there still rest in the broken
Tumulus ashes and charred
Bones thrown in a corner by
Grave robbers, now just as dead?
She was once a shining flower
With eyebrows like the first night's moon,
Her white face, her brocaded
Robes perfumed with cypress and
Sandalwood; she sang in the Court
Before the Emperor, songs
Of China and Turkestan.
She served him wine in a cup
Of silver and pearls, that gleamed
Like the moonlight on her sleeves.
A young girl with black hair
Longer than her white body—
Who never grew old. Now owls
And nightjars sing in a mist
Of silver and pearls.

The wheel
Swings and turns counterclockwise.
The old graspings live again
In the new consequences.
Yet, still, I walk this same path
Above my cabin in warm
Moonlit mist, in rain, in
Autumn wind and rain of maple
Leaves, in spring rain of cherry
Blossoms, in new snow deeper
Than my clogs. And tonight in
Midsummer, a night enclosed
In an infinite pearl.
Ninety-nine nights over

Yamashina Pass, and the
Hundredth night and the first night
Are the same night. The night
Known prior to consciousness,
Night of ecstasy, night of
Illumination so complete
It cannot be called perceptible.

Winter, the flowers sleep on
The branches. Spring, they awake
And open to probing bees.
Summer, unborn flowers sleep
In the young seeds ripening
In the fruit. The mountain pool
Is invisible in the
Glowing mist. But the mist-drowned
Moon overhead is visible
Drowned in the invisible water.

Mist-drenched, moonlit, the sculpture
Of an orb spider glitters
Across the path. I walk around
Through the bamboo grass. The mist
Dissolves everything else, the
Living and the dead, except
This occult mathematics of light.
Nothing moves. The wind that blows
Down the mountain slope from
The pass and scatters the spring
Blossoms and the autumn leaves
Is still tonight. Even the
Spider's net of jewels has ceased
To tremble. I look back at
An architecture of pearls
And silver wire. Each minute
Droplet reflects a moon, as
Once did the waterpails of
Matsukaze and Murasame.

And I realize that this
Transcendent architecture
Lost in the forest where no one passes
Is itself the Net of Indra,
The compound infinities of infinities,
The Flower Wreath,
Each universe reflecting
Every other, reflecting
Itself from every other,
And the moon the single thought
That populates the Void.
The night grows still more still. No
Sound at all, only a flute
Playing soundlessly in the
Circle of dancing gopis.

THE LOVE POEMS OF
MARICHIKO

*translated by Kenneth Rexroth*

*To Marichiko*
*Kenneth Rexroth*

*To Kenneth Rexroth*
*Marichiko*

# I

I sit at my desk.
What can I write to you?
Sick with love,
I long to see you in the flesh.
I can write only,
"I love you. I love you. I love you."
Love cuts through my heart
And tears my vitals.
Spasms of longing suffocate me
And will not stop.

# II

If I thought I could get away
And come to you,
Ten thousand miles would be like one mile.
But we are both in the same city
And I dare not see you,
And a mile is longer than a million miles.

## III

Oh the anguish of these secret meetings
In the depth of night,
I wait with the shoji open.
You come late, and I see your shadow
Move through the foliage
At the bottom of the garden.
We embrace—hidden from my family.
I weep into my hands.
My sleeves are already damp.
We make love, and suddenly
The fire watch loom up
With clappers and lantern.
How cruel they are
To appear at such a moment.
Upset by their apparition,
I babble nonsense
And can't stop talking
Words with no connection.

## I V

You ask me what I thought about
Before we were lovers.
The answer is easy.
Before I met you
I didn't have anything to think about.

## V

Autumn covers all the world
With Chinese old brocade.
The crickets cry, "We mend old clothes."
They are more thrifty than I am.

# VI

Just us.
In our little house
Far from everybody,
Far from the world,
Only the sound of water over stone.
And then I say to you,
"Listen. Hear the wind in the trees."


# VII

Making love with you
Is like drinking sea water.
The more I drink
The thirstier I become,
Until nothing can slake my thirst
But to drink the entire sea.

# VIII

A single ray in the dawn,
The bliss of our love
Is incomprehensible.
No sun shines there, no
Moon, no stars, no lightning flash,
Not even lamplight.
All things are incandescent
With love which lights up all the world.

## IX

You wake me,
Part my thighs, and kiss me.
I give you the dew
Of the first morning of the world.

## X

Frost covers the reeds of the marsh.
A fine haze blows through them,
Crackling the long leaves.
My full heart throbs with bliss.

## XI

Uguisu sing in the blossoming trees.
Frogs sing in the green rushes.
Everywhere the same call
Of being to being.
Somber clouds waver in the void.
Fishing boats waver in the tide.
Their sails carry them out.
But ropes, as of old, woven
With the hair of their women,
Pull them back
Over their reflections on the green depths,
To the ports of love.

## XII

Come to me, as you come
Softly to the rose bed of coals
Of my fireplace
Glowing through the night-bound forest.

## XIII

Lying in the meadow, open to you
Under the noon sun,
Hazy smoke half hides
My rose petals.

# XIV

On the bridges
And along the banks
Of Kamo River, the crowds
Watch the character "Great"
Burst into red fire on the mountain
And at last die out.
Your arm about me,
I burn with passion.
Suddenly I realize—
It is life I am burning with.
These hands burn,
Your arm about me burns,
And look at the others,
All about us in the crowd, thousands,
They are all burning—
Into embers and then into darkness.
I am happy.
Nothing of mine is burning.

## XV

Because I dream
Of you every night,
My lonely days
Are only dreams.

## XVI

Scorched with love, the cicada
Cries out. Silent as the firefly,
My flesh is consumed with love.

## XVII

Let us sleep together here tonight.
Tomorrow, who knows where we will sleep?
Maybe tomorrow we will lie in the fields,
Our heads on the rocks.

## XVIII

Fires
Burn in my heart.
No smoke rises.
No one knows.

## XIX

I pass the day tense, day-
Dreaming of you. I relax with joy
When in the twilight I hear
The evening bells ring from temple to temple.


## XX

Who is there? Me.
Me who? I am me. You are you.
You take my pronoun,
And we are us.

## XXI

The full moon of Spring
Rises from the Void,
And pushes aside the net
Of stars, a pure crystal ball
On pale velvet, set with gems.


## XXII

This Spring, Mercury
Is farthest from the sun and
Burns, a ray of light,
In the glow of dawn
Over the uncountable
Sands and waves of the
Illimitable ocean.

## XXIII

I wish I could be
Kannon of eleven heads
To kiss you, Kannon
Of the thousand arms,
To embrace you forever.


## XXIV

I scream as you bite
My nipples, and orgasm
Drains my body, as if I
Had been cut in two.

## XXV

Your tongue thrums and moves
Into me, and I become
Hollow and blaze with
Whirling light, like the inside
Of a vast expanding pearl.

## XXVI

It is the time when
The wild geese return. Between
The setting sun and
The rising moon, a line of
Brant write the character "heart."

## XXVII

As I came from the
Hot bath, you took me before
The horizontal mirror
Beside the low bed, while my
Breasts quivered in your hands, my
Buttocks shivered against you.


## XXVIII

Spring is early this year.
Laurel, plums, peaches,
Almonds, mimosa,
All bloom at once. Under the
Moon, night smells like your body.

## XXIX

Love me. At this moment we
Are the happiest
People in the world.

## XXX

Nothing in the world is worth
One sixteenth part of the love
Which sets free our hearts.
Just as the Morning Star in
The dark before dawn
Lights up the world with its ray,
So love shines in our hearts and
Fills us with glory.

## XXXI

Some day in six inches of
Ashes will be all
That's left of our passionate minds,
Of all the world created
By our love, its origin
And passing away.


## XXXII

I hold your head tight between
My thighs, and press against your
Mouth, and float away
Forever, in an orchid
Boat on the River of Heaven.

## XXXIII

I cannot forget
The perfumed dusk inside the
Tent of my black hair,
As we awoke to make love
After a long night of love.

## XXXIV

Every morning, I
Wake alone, dreaming my
Arm is your sweet flesh
Pressing my lips.

## XXXV

The uguisu sleeps in the bamboo grove,
One night a man traps her in a bamboo trap,
Now she sleeps in a bamboo cage.


## XXXVI

I am sad this morning.
The fog was so dense,
I could not see your shadow
As you passed my shoji.

## XXXVII

Is it just the wind
In the bamboo grass,
Or are you coming?
At the least sound
My heart skips a beat.
I try to suppress my torment
And get a little sleep,
But I only become more restless.

## XXXVIII

I waited all night.
By midnight I was on fire.
In the dawn, hoping
To find a dream of you,
I laid my weary head
On my folded arms,
But the songs of the waking
Birds tormented me.

## XXXIX

Because I can't stop,
Even for a moment's rest from
Thinking of you,
The obi which wound around me twice,
Now goes around me three times.


## XL

As the wheel follows the hoof
Of the ox that pulls the cart,
My sorrow follows your footsteps,
As you leave me in the dawn.

## XLI

On the mountain,
Tiring to the feet,
Lost in the fog, the pheasant
Cries out, seeking her mate.


## XLII

How many lives ago
I first entered the torrent of love,
At last to discover
There is no further shore.
Yet I know I will enter again and again.

## XLIII

Two flowers in a letter.
The moon sinks into the far off hills.
Dew drenches the bamboo grass.
I wait.
Crickets sing all night in the pine tree.
At midnight the temple bells ring.
Wild geese cry overhead.
Nothing else.

## XLIV

The disorder of my hair
Is due to my lonely sleepless pillow.
My hollow eyes and gaunt cheeks
Are your fault.

## XLV

When in the Noh theater
We watched Shizuka Gozen
Trapped in the snow,
I enjoyed the tragedy,
For I thought,
Nothing like this
Will ever happen to me.


## XLVI

Emitting a flood of light,
Flooded with light within,
Our love was dimmed by
Forces which came from without.

## XLVII

How long, long ago.
By the bridge at Uji,
In our little boat,
We swept through clouds of fireflies.

## XLVIII

Now the fireflies of our youth
Are all gone,
Thanks to the efficient insecticides
Of our middle age.

## XLIX

Once again I hear
The first frogs sing in the pond.
I am overwhelmed by the past.

## L

In the park a crow awakes
And cries out under the full moon,
And I awake and sob
For the years that are gone.

## LI

Did you take me because you loved me?
Did you take me without love?
Or did you just take me
To experiment on my heart?

## LII

Once I shone afar like a
Snow-covered mountain.
Now I am lost like
An arrow shot in the dark.
He is gone and I must learn
To live alone and
Sleep alone like a hermit
Buried deep in the jungle.
I shall learn to go
Alone, like the unicorn.

## LIII

Without me you can only
Live at random like
A falling pachinko ball.
I am your wisdom.


## LIV

Did a cuckoo cry?
I look out, but there is only dawn and
The moon in its final night.
Did the moon cry out
Horobirete! Horobirete!
Perishing! Perishing!

## L V

The night is too long to the sleepless.
The road is too long to the footsore.
Life is too long to a woman
Made foolish by passion.
Why did I find a crooked guide
On the twisted paths of love?

## L V I

This flesh you have loved
Is fragile, unstable by nature
As a boat adrift.
The fires of the cormorant fishers
Flare in the night.
My heart flares with this agony.
Do you understand?
My life is going out.
Do you understand?
My life.
Vanishing like the stakes
That hold the nets against the current
In Uji River, the current and the mist
Are taking me.

## LVII

Night without end. Loneliness.
The wind has driven a maple leaf
Against the shoji. I wait, as in the old days,
In our secret place, under the full moon.
The last bell crickets sing.
I found your old love letters,
Full of poems you never published.
Did it matter? They were only for me.

## LVIII

Half in a dream
I become aware
That the voices of the crickets
Grow faint with the growing Autumn.
I mourn for this lonely
Year that is passing
And my own being
Grows fainter and fades away.

## L I X

I hate this shadow of a ghost
Under the full moon.
I run my fingers through my greying hair,
And wonder, have I grown so thin?


## L X

Chilled through, I wake up
With the first light. Outside my window
A red maple leaf floats silently down.
What am I to believe?
Indifference?
Malice?
I hate the sight of coming day
Since that morning when
Your insensitive gaze turned me to ice
Like the pale moon in the dawn.

# NOTES

## On Flower Wreath Hill

In 1974–75, we lived in Kyoto in an embayment of Higashi-yama, the Eastern Hills, in a seven hundred year old farm house. The range, which rises directly above the easternmost long street of the city, culminates in Mt. Hiei. It is almost entirely forest and wildlife reserve because scattered all through it are temples and tombs and cemeteries. Our street led up to Yama-shina Pass and across the street from our house a shoulder of the range rose abruptly to a little plateau on which long ago had been built the tumulus of a princess which now is only an irregular heap of low mounds covered with trees. Behind it is the complex of Shingon Temples called Sennuji, which includes a large building in which are stored the ashes of former emperors. The Japanese seldom bury the dead, and the tumulus age was of very short duration at the beginning of Japanese history, although it resulted in immense keyhole shaped mounds, one of them of greater bulk than the Great Pyramid of Gizeh, keyhole shaped and surrounded by a moat. The one mentioned in the poem had been a far more modest structure. Mt. Hiei is the site of the founding temples of Tendai and once, before they were all slaughtered by Nobunaga, contained sixty thousand monks at least. Today there are still many monasteries—but also an amusement park. Kamo River flows close to the edge of the mountains.

The second and third verses of Part II are a conflation of well-known classic Japanese poems, and Part V is entirely so.

Tanabata is Seven-Seven, the seventh day of the seventh month, when the Cowboy, Altair, crosses the Milky Way to lie for one night only with the Weaving Girl, Vega. Magpies link wings and form a bridge for him to cross, but there are many Chinese and Japanese dawn poems which would indicate that he rowed himself back.

Kegonkyo (Flower Wreath Sutra) is the Avatamsaka Sutra, by far the most profound and the most mystical of the sutras of Mahavana.

Before he entered Paranirvana, Buddha said, "The combinations of the world are unstable by nature. Monks, strive without ceasing."

St. Elmo's fires are the glowing balls of atmospheric electricity that usually appear as tips of light on the extremities of pointed objects such as church towers or airplane wings during stormy weather.

Important Japanese graves or family burial lots (only the ashes are buried) are often marked by a stupa (Japanese: *sotoba*) consisting of four and sometimes five stones, a cube, a sphere, a lune, a triangle, and sometimes a little shape on top of the triangle. Amongst other things, they symbolize the elements: earth, water, air, fire, and what we used to call ether. Unstable by nature, they do not take many decades to fall apart. There is a Mahayana doctrine, Sunyata, that ultimate reality is Void Only and what seems like reality are only fleeting compounds.

The third verse paragraph of Part VIII begins the possession by Ono no Komachi continued in the next paragraph, and there are many echoes of the three great Noh plays on Komachi, the greatest Japanese woman poet.

The fifth paragraph opens with an echo of a commentary on the Lotus Sutra; but with the orb spider's net, it becomes a poem of the Flower Wreath Sutra, known in Hinduism as the Net of Indra. Matsukaze and Murasame were two lovers of a prince exiled to the shore of Suma. They were salt girls who evaporated sea water over burning dried seaweed and driftwood, and who saw the moon one night after the prince had left, each in her own water pail or pails. There is a very beautiful Noh play on the subject, and they are common dolls. As dolls, they each carry two pails on a yoke and the classic dance with the yoked pails is one of the most beautiful.

The gopis are the nineteen thousand milkmaids who dance to Krishna's flute. His flute music connects true reality and the gopis, who dance and become Real. Music is being, but behind being is Ishvara, what Western philosophy would call the Absolute behind all absolutes. Kabbalah calls it the Ayn Soph and Buddhism the Adi-buddha. As the music enters her, and she enters the dance, each gopi knows that she is Radha, the beloved of Krishna, his Shakti, his Power, or his Prajna, his Wisdom. He is the avatar of Vishnu, and power and wisdom are the same. The Vishnulila, the play of Vishnu with the world of illusion.

Modern stuffy Indian pundits say that Krishna didn't really make love to nineteen thousand milkmaids. He knew by heart 19,000 slokas of the Vedas.

Flower Wreath Hill is also a Chinese and Japanese euphemism for a cemetery.

# The Love Poems of Marichiko

Marichiko is the pen name of a contemporary young woman who lives near the temple of Marishi-ben in Kyoto.

Marishi-ben is an Indian, pre-Aryan, goddess of the dawn who is a bodhisattva in Buddhism and patron of geisha, prostitutes, women in childbirth, and lovers, and, in another aspect, once of samurai. Few temples or shrines to her or even statues exist in Japan, but her presence is indicated by statues, often in avenues like sphinxes, of wild boars, who also draw her chariot. She has three faces: the front of compassion; one side, a sow; the other a woman in ecstasy. She is a popular, though hidden, deity of tantric, Tachigawa Shingon. As the Ray of Light, the Shakti, or Prajna, the Power or Wisdom of Vairocana (the primordial Buddha, Dainichi Nyorai), she is seated on his lap in sexual bliss, Myōjō—the Morning Star.

Marichiko writes me, now that I am doing so many of her poems, in reference to the note on her in my *One Hundred More Poems from the Japanese*, "Although Marichi is the Shakti, or power, of the Indian god of the sun, she is the Prajna, or wisdom, of Dainichi Nyorai. Dainichi means Great Sun, but he is that only in a metaphorical sense, the Illuminator of the compound infinity of infinities of universes. The Buddhas and Bodhisattvas of Mahayana do not have Shaktis as consorts, for the simple reason that there is no such thing as power in Buddhism. Power is ignorance and grasping. With illumination, it turns into wisdom."

Notice, that like the English seventeenth-century poet Rochester, many of her poems turn religious verse into erotic, and she also turns traditional geisha songs into visionary poems. They therefore bear comparison with Persian Sufi poets, Hafidh, Attar, Sa'adi, and others, and with the Arab, Ibn el Arabi—with all of whom she is familiar in translation.

The series of poems, as should be obvious, form a sort of little novel and recall the famous *Diary of Izumi Shikibu* without the connecting prose. Notice that the sex of the lover is ambiguous.

Poem IV. Echoes Fujiwara no Atsutada, "Ai minto no."

Poem V. Narihira compares the leaf covered water of Tatsuta River to Chinese old brocade.

Poem VI. Echoes several "honeymoon houses," the modern one by Yosano Akiko.

Poem VII. Echoes a passage in the *Katha Upanishad*.

Poem VIII. Echoes a passage in the *Katha Upanishad*.

Poem XI. The uguisu, often translated "nightingale," is not a nightingale and does not sing at night. It is the Japanese bush warbler, *Horeites cantans cantans*, or *Cettia diphone*.

Poem XIV. Refers to the Festival, Daimonji Okuribi, sending of the dead back to heaven, when huge bonfires in the shape of characters are lit on the mountain sides around Kyoto. There is a paraphrase of Buddha's Fire Sermon and a paraphrase of Rilke's paraphrase of that.

Poem XVI. Based on a geisha song in many forms.

Poem XVII. Either the poem on Hitomaro's (Japan's greatest poet—b.?–d.739) death or his own poem on a friend's death.

Poem XX. This poem, though syntactically barely possible, would be inconceivable in classical Japanese.

Poem XXI. There is an implied reference to the doctrine of Void Only and then to the Avatamsaka Sutra (Kegongyo) as the Net of Indra.

Poem XXII. The ray of light of the Morning Star—Marishiten—Myogo.

Poem XXIII. Both forms of Kannon (Avalokitesvara) are common statues. Sanjusangendo, across from the Kyoto Art Museum, is a hall of over a thousand such, each very slightly different.

Poem XXVI. Brant, *Branta bernicia* is Japanese Koku-gan, are small, dark geese, who winter in the north of Honshu, the main island. Unlike many birds of the family, they do not fly in arrow formations, but in an irregular line.

Poem XXVII. The horizontal mirror is a narrow mirror, closed by sliding panels, alongside the bed in many Japanese inns (ryokan). Shunga erotic woodblock prints, representing them, are usually called "seen through the slats of a bamboo screen" by Westerners—Japanese until recent times had nothing resembling our venetian blinds.

Poem XXX. Echoes the Buddhist sutra Itivuttaka, III, 7.

Poem XXXI. Echoes the Buddhist sutra, Samyutta Nikaya, II, 3, 8.

Poem XXXII. "Orchid boat" is a metaphor for the female sexual organ.

Poem XXXIII. Echoes Yosano Akiko.

Poem XXXVI. Shoji—sliding doors or windows with "panes" of paper.

Poem XXXVIII. Ono no Komachi (834–880) is certainly Japan's greatest woman poet. Marichiko echoes her most famous poem—"Hito no awan/Tsuki no naki ni wa/Omoiokite/Mune hashibiri ni/Kokoro yakeori."

Poem XL. Echoes the first lines of the Dhammapada, the ancient popular exposition of Theravada Buddhism.

Poem XLI. Echoes an anonymous poem usually attributed to Hitomaro.

Poem XLII. Echoes a Buddhist sutra.

Poem XLIV. There are a great many midaregami, "tangled hair" poems, from an exchange between Mikata and his wife in the *Manyoshu*—eighth century—to the first great book of Yosano Akiko, called *Midaregami*, the early twentieth-century woman poet and still the unequalled poet of modern verse in classical (tanka) form.

Poem XLV. Shizuka Gozen (twelfth century) was a white dress dancer of spectacular beauty who became the lover of Minamoto no Yoshitsune, the tragic hero of the epic of the war between the Taira and Minamoto, which brought to an end the great years of early Japanese civilization. He was the principal general of his brother Yoritomo, and broke the power of the Taira in a series of battles. After Yoritomo outlawed his brother, Shizuka was captured fleeing through the snowbound wilderness on Mt. Yoshino. When Yorimoto and his courtiers were worshipping at the Tsuruga-Oka Shrine at Kamakura, he commanded Shizuka to perform her most famous dance. She refused but was finally forced to dance. Shortly after, she gave birth to Yoshitsune's son, whom Yoritomo murdered. She then became a Buddhist nun and lived to an old age, long after Yoshitsune had been destroyed in his refuge in the far North. She is not a great

143

poet but, with Yoshitsune, one of the tragic figures of Japanese history. Her dance occurs in several Noh plays.

Poem XLVI. Echoes a Buddhist sutra, but also refers to herself as Marichi—Ray of Light—and Dainichi (Vairocana)—The Transcedent Sun.

Poems XLVII–XLVIII. These two poems are factual—D.D.T. exterminated most of the fireflies of Japan, and the Hotaru Matsuri—Firefly Festivals—are no longer held, or even remembered by the younger generation.

Poem LII. Echoes a Buddhist sutra, the poems of Yokobue and her lover in the *Heike Monogatori*, and finally Buddha's Unicorn (often called "Rhinoceros") Sermon.

Poem LIII. Pachinko is a form of vertical pinball—and immense pachinko parlors, crowded with hypnotized players, litter Japan. It is a symbol of total immersion in the world of illusion, ignorance, suffering, and grasping. Wisdom is Prajna— the female consort of a Buddha in esoteric Shingon Buddhism, corresponding to the Shakti, power, the consort of a Hindu god. Note that Prajna is, in a sense, the contradictory of Shakti.

Poem LIV. The first cuckoo in the dawn poem probably dates back before the *Kokinshu*, the second Imperial Anthology. There are many geisha songs that essentially repeat it. But Marichiko says, "was it the moon itself that cried out?" a completely novel last line. The hototogisu does not say "cuckoo," but something like the five syllables of its name, or "horobirete," perishing. It is *Cuculus poliocephalus*.

Poem LV. Echoes a Buddhist sutra.

Poem LVII. The bell cricket is the Tsukutsuku boshi, *Cosmopsal tria colorata*.

As I finish these notes, I realize that, whereas Westerners, alienated from their own culture, embrace Zen Buddhism, most young Japanese consider it reactionary, the religion of the officer caste, the great rich, and foreign hippies. There is however a growing movement of appreciation of Theravada (Hinayana) Buddhism, hitherto hardly known except to scholars in Japan. Marichiko's poems are deeply influenced by Theravada suttas, Tachigawa Shingon, folksongs, Yosano Akiko, and the great women poets of Heian Japan—Ono no Komachi, Murasaki Shikibu, and Izumi Shikibu.

# INDEX OF TITLES, FIRST LINES, & AUTHORS TRANSLATED

Poem titles are printed in *italic* type, names of authors translated are in LARGE AND SMALL capital letters.

145

# New Directions Paperbooks – A Partial Listing

For complete listing request free catalog from
New Directions, 80 Eighth Avenue, New York 10011          † Bilingual

For complete listing request free catalog from
New Directions, 80 Eighth Avenue, New York 10011

† Bilingual